something has to happen next

andrew michael roberts

something has to happen next

university of iowa press, iowa city

ISBN-13: 978-1-58729-794-6
ISBN-10: 1-58729-794-9
LCCN: 2008935530

09 10 11 12 13 P 5 4 3 2 1

for jackie hanzal

contents

· ·

2. something has to happen next

acknowledgments

Grateful acknowledgment to the following
journals in which some poems in this
collection originally appeared: "lamb" in
Burnside Review; "california" in *Cincinnati
Review*; "the story of my beard" in *Colorado
Review*; "somewhere a buried bone awaits"
in *Fugue*.

Some of the poems in this collection appeared
in the chapbook *Dear Wild Abandon*,
published by the Poetry Society of America
in 2008.

The line "in the night of the womb the spirit
quickens into flesh" is borrowed from John
G. Neihardt's *Black Elk Speaks*.

Thanks to the following people whose support
helped greatly in the creation of this book:
Dara Wier, James Tate, Amy Dickinson,
Tony Wolk, Carol Franks, Dani Blackman,
Andre Kahlil, Jeannie Hoag, Emily Renaud,
Peggy Woods, Phil Moll, Chuck Boyer,
Brent Goeres, Tim Roberts, Mike and Celia
Roberts, and Jackie Hanzal.

dear wild abandon,

dear wild abandon,

you little
time

bomb.

i've crept close and touched you
in your pregnant sleep

with the flame
of my tongue.

if i bite
and swallow, would you

explode in me?

we are not birds

. . . .

this beautiful speed will be the end of us.
those are stars in our teeth.

explain yourself

my life was like this when i found it.
so i walked with it the entire way.
the chickens followed, they are not mine.

i found you feathered at the small of the back
among honeycomb and thunderstorms.
you blinked, and a galaxy
spun to life.
you'd caught a comet
that blazed from your beak
at the end of its mad tail.

poem written on the mirror of her skin

each illuminated breath
is the moon
slipping inside itself.

dear man on fire,

. . . .

you beautiful
waste.

don't die out,

don't go too soon
to dark smoke like arms

flung over the city's
face,

wretched home
to all our eyes.

tragic figure in a rearview

took a hammer
to my windshield.
now a cobweb
sprawls between the future
and me.
it's gorgeous,
its translucence,
the prismal sun
I don't
deserve.

the moon

. . . .

all the other moons
get their own names.

what i know of the moon

. . . .

i am only half myself.
the other side's
a dark idea
i like to believe in.

strip mall

. . . .

we stop to watch
seagulls swarm
the Burger King.

birds of paradise

across the desert we kissed
and dreamt one-legged of islands.
we were not yet home,
a sea of buffaloes
carried us on its back.

before sleep takes us

i memorize my life
so it's still there
when i arrive again
in the morning.

swallows built their nest around it

. . . .

she slings it
on a limb,
climbs up to
sew tiny lights
inside.
the pulse,
the half-moon behind it.
you can smell
the coming
snow.

when we were giant

in time we grew
tall enough
to hear
the lost tiny geese honk
to be let out
of the atmosphere.

again i strike your window in full flight

. . . .

i've dreamt of fingers
and their intricate instruments,

someone to carry me
room to room

while i sing.

dear artificial heart,

at the silent edge
of sleep i hear

your perfect plastic
gaskets clap and know

i'm more
than half alive.

my blood a little lost
in your strange rooms,

this empty house
too much for me.

the moon out there like ice,
a warning hung

above the artificial
earth.

pledge of allegiance

. . . .

i have a wig i do not wear.
it is the shape of my country at night
and mewls for me to lift it
from its cold hook.

the face of jesus in my bite bruise

your holy teeth singing
the life story of my skin.

and the stars,
the broken ones that let go

and fell through the ceiling
of my eyes.

laundromat at the end of the world

you can feel
the gravity growing.
the washers shake their chains
and squeal.
something in me
says that man's
got a gun in his coat.
he's ready
when the storm
throws open the door
and shoots its hail in
sideways to make way
for the moon
crashing down.

dear special theory of relativity,

please accept our sincere apologies.
nothing's relative since you've been gone,

the sunbeams halted
halfway down the sky,

the long train of cars dead
in the street, blurry from the rush

of trees racing past
on their way to work.

you can hear it through the cumulative heartbeats

. . . .

you, and a skyful of swallows
schooling like fish.
then the planets' heavy whir
through space.

you never touched me

you've seen me in the chickencoop
feeling for eggs. not the eggs,
but the warm bellies, the sharp
protective pecks at the bones of my hands.

they molt in hopes of airier plumage

was it me running nude
in the woods of my youth
who gave birds
their crazy dream?

dear quark,

. . . .

now i know you,
i see you
everywhere

as if you've jumped
the long green train
of my eye,

little tramp.

prove you wrong

· ·

i'm doing two-knuckle push-ups
in the driveway.
there's a black shape of me
where it hasn't yet snowed.

the end

. . . .

it was the end of something,
and so we grew sad
according to how much we'd loved it.
now, nothing
but our great variety of sadnesses
and for some
a seed of instinct suggesting
something else
may eventually begin.

dear catastrophe,

. . . .

the answer: we were not
thinking anything.

we might have known you
by the wind's lying down

like shadows beside us,
by the static and the starlings' dead silence.

something has to happen next

rehearsal

here is a sparrow bone to stand in for me.
carry it like the look you gave
when you wanted me unclothed
in meadows under the meteorites.
when your feverish hips kept winter at bay
with the skinny trees at the far dark edge.
take me in a finger's sweep. tie me
with hair and watch the knots
unwind. there is a trick to everything.
sometimes you have to put it to your tongue
to know it from its deep desire.
my question is when
am i perfect, and will you
be looking the other way.

this or something like it

here is the sound of the heel
of a hammer and the sea
escaping an oyster shell.
someone's standing on the shoulders
of barnacles to smash a lovely
life. sometimes you know
exactly what to do.
between strikes a silence settles in.
down the reach, a pregnant dog
lies down in the surf.
dark islands in the distance,
two crows smug in a dead fir tree.
this stone in your hand's
the size of their skulls.
you can feel your lungs and know
you're alive. something
has to happen next. with its stare
the half moon draws the sea
like a lover and makes you
seem as small as you are.

a cyclist passes with a cello on his back

. . . .

we bring our birds
to cafés in toy cages.
a few crumbs tossed in
among the husks while we sit.
they do all the talking.
when we go we always leave
a sip of tea in the cup.

lamb

god forgets. he leaves the iron on and your beautiful city
burns to the ground. god touches you and you are it.
alone in a desert of ash is a difficult game to win. home
base is flame and smoke. once god said hunger. once
he said fuck, and how could we tell him
we'd figured it out on our own.
i'm waiting, god, for a watermelon. say pomegranate.
say city, say rib. an armadillo to sniff at my feet. it's
armor and nothing else. let's lift it like a mirror.
put it to my ear like a shell. god puts the ocean
in an armadillo shell. it rattles of whalebones. i remember
water, but all the cacti are black. all the sand
is glass beneath the ash, a calm buried sea.
god descends the sky like a spider. i can feel it.
he is everywhere, twiddling his thumbs.
i think he's waiting for me.

the story of my beard

in my beard, a trailer park,
a cyclone fence, a forest.
dumpsters the skinny trash bears
sneak out to root through at night.
their claws cast sparks. lightbulbs,
porkbones. aerosol cans they eat
and explode. in my beard, army tanks.
the thunder of anti-aircraft artillery.
everything's blue from the trailers'
tvs. blue soldiers, blue birds building nests
in the still-tepid barrels.
in my beard, the children are nothing.
they leave their bikes piled up
on the street. they run to the woods
to play war within war. blue bullets
rip through the chokecherry leaves.
home base is an exploded bear
to be beaten with sticks.
home is a foxhole you dug through the roots.
blue mound of dirt piled up at its lip.
in my beard, from above, a forest
of dark foxholes. inside each
like a seed, a sleeping child waiting
to be kissed and tucked in.

. . . .

the mustachioed one's
childless

and hard
on the buses.

when he
brakes

they
scream.

winter museum

on one wall,
a window.

nothing out there
but a light snow

collecting in the shapes
of our names.

what we know

weren't we superheroes, love-
smug, white-caped in wet snow,

braving the blizzard arm
in arm, invincible—

until the geese, half-buried,
half-asleep in paired mounds

honked softly hill to hill
as if answering

from the warm perfect faith
of their being.

the moments before the crash landing are clearest

. . . .

i woke without you and the igloo
seeming colder. i could peek
out the crawl-hole but if the entire
spinning earth's imaginary i don't want to know.
i have my pelts and visions
of you asleep in your summer skin loving
the deep heart of a tall grass prairie.
i have polar bears and snow
blindness. you have sunsets
striking the silent crows iridescent.
when they swoon to their own new beauty
and the chorus frogs kick in, do you think
of me thinking of you thinking of me?
i tell you what. if i had an albatross
i'd let it lift me like a message
to the jet stream just as the toothy flows
ingest our empty love-shell. you would know me
by the touch of ice on the tongue
of the wind. you would wait with a bouquet
of black feathers and the rest of
our story still warm on your lips.

serendipity

the violins hiving like bees in us
betray our bittersweet hello.

we smoke like signals
from the friction and things

begin to shower down.
for us, birds drop

backwards from their branches,
a whistling blanket of heart-

beats to bury the loving.
tonight, the meteorites.

later, the sea,
our little strings singing

to the astonishment
of lovesick whales.

safe shower

my cap is
    a condom

stretched over my head.

we're ready,
she

in her snorkel
and pink

water-wings.

stalactite

hang
on

little tooth,

said
the mountain

drawing strings
of bats like

a chirping
black
floss.

not physics, but loosed dogs who lick the earth
and make us spin. lost dogs, always
almost catching their own dark tails in their teeth.
so we are dizzy and don't know it,
and this is the story of time. look
inside a spider's web and see. that constellation
of dew is eyes shaking in their silk sockets
to the thundering footpads. touch one.
reach through and pat the happy panting head
of night. beyond the sun, a long black pelt
stretched over the bones of dead stars.
one velvet ear is eons. when you die
you curl up in it and they just keep running.
you can hear the click of claws tectonic.
even from sleep you hear the bright blinding howls
and believe they are dreams.

for the dispossessed

so we sleep in the river.
the barely-touched. thirsty to the stones
of our eyes for an intimacy like that.
some endless licking thing to talk us
from the shallows and make
us glow from the strange collected light.
to that tongue we are accidental.
we slip away. finally, we flake
like scales and shine.
you may remember us. from your sleep
you may surface with a fist of silt
and find just what you expected.

**in the night of the womb the spirit
quickens into flesh**

. . . .

and so i
am nocturnal
gnawing big-eyed

at the moonlit years
with the wolves
and moths

while night
and its toothy stars
nibble me slowly

into shadow.
white day is for
others.

mother i am
not lonely,
i am nearly

the dark space
between the sun
and itself.

coyotes

. . . .

one pain,
these howls

we hurl at the arc-
ed bone of her.

how
careless,

she turns
the mist

to impossible
milk.

how untouchable
her far

cold love.

chosen

one night i went that way with a pack of dogs.
beyond the streetlights.
we glistened,
we were dead set on it,
no one stopping to sniff
or lift a leg
to what was already forgotten.

world,

. . . .

just where
would you be—

and where
do you think
you're going—

without
me?

levitator's apprentice

i dream you who sleep
standing up like horses.

man of the year

trombones always swooned for you.
it was july with green twilight inking in
and the feeding bats missing us by inches.
you were dancing with the long train
of your beard thick in your hands
as a river of birds. they grazed soundlessly.
how handsome, our envy. our star-
speckled melancholy. we could only stand
in our clothes and be ourselves.
what a relief, your fingers
spelling our gently dressed nudity.
when you snapped them: carolina
parakeets. like sparks the fledglings spat
from your handsome arms
into the darkening green as if
they'd never been forgotten.

california

if you are mountainous, immovable, stand here
and stare down the san andreas fault. stand
statuesque at big sur and look west,
wait for gray whales to sneak past, smuggling
their songs like a secret you don't deserve.
from the bluffs you are indecipherable.
turn and walk inland and grow larger
in your mind. the highway, the headlands,
a slug on the trail you can step over
and feel saved. coyotes and car motors.
a howl deep in the engines of your bones.
they will move you. somewhere in the past,
a lost lighthouse and a stair that disappears
into the surf at high tide. ahead, the wild
dogs of california crying the sun's slow death.
they are always further off. if you are marvelous,
follow them. in the dark their eyes
like a new city scatter among the hills.
this is your city.

if nothing else

. . . .

remember winter by the way
the puddles froze around their trash
and became beautiful. useless,
how the skinny crows starved
scratching at their mirrors.
did we love enough, barefoot in our
nest of broken grass blades.
at the edge of a forest
didn't we drive through a deer's
lingering breath and forget everything.
someday we're forgiven i think.
i always wanted you with
the cold green feathers of your iris
folded back, waiting for the first
fingers of sun. you were busy watching out
the window past the antlerish limbs
where you thought your shadow should be.

listen

oh the smalls of their backs.
how they break under
your kiss of smoke and cedar boughs.
press your ear to another
and you will understand.
how you become nothing
in the taking. how there you are,
thirsty with the hills in the distance,
growing quieter the closer you come.

i'll pack a pretty shirt

lay me here in bluestem and baptisia
and listen with your ear against
the bowing wind. the day wants nothing
but our long quiet looks.
do you hear the clovers closing
soft as eyes. i could kiss you blindly.
tell me something. nearly touch me
as the sun forgets itself
and sets on a shoulder blade.
this is what i remember.

IOWA POETRY PRIZE AND EDWIN FORD PIPER POETRY AWARD WINNERS

. . . .

1987
Elton Glaser, *Tropical Depressions*
Michael Pettit, *Cardinal Points*

1988
Bill Knott, *Outremer*
Mary Ruefle, *The Adamant*

1989
Conrad Hilberry, *Sorting the Smoke*
Terese Svoboda, *Laughing Africa*

1990
Philip Dacey, *Night Shift at the Crucifix Factory*
Lynda Hull, *Star Ledger*

1991
Greg Pape, *Sunflower Facing the Sun*
Walter Pavlich, *Running near the End of the World*

1992
Lola Haskins, *Hunger*
Katherine Soniat, *A Shared Life*

1993
Tom Andrews, *The Hemophiliac's Motorcycle*
Michael Heffernan, *Love's Answer*
John Wood, *In Primary Light*

1994
James McKean, *Tree of Heaven*
Bin Ramke, *Massacre of the Innocents*
Ed Roberson, *Voices Cast Out to Talk Us In*

1995
Ralph Burns, *Swamp Candles*
Maureen Seaton, *Furious Cooking*

1996
Pamela Alexander, *Inland*
Gary Gildner, *The Bunker in the Parsley Fields*
John Wood, *The Gates of the Elect Kingdom*

1997
Brendan Galvin, *Hotel Malabar*
Leslie Ullman, *Slow Work through Sand*

1998
Kathleen Peirce, *The Oval Hour*
Bin Ramke, *Wake*
Cole Swensen, *Try*

1999
Larissa Szporluk, *Isolato*
Liz Waldner, *A Point Is That Which Has No Part*

2000
Mary Leader, *The Penultimate Suitor*

2001
Joanna Goodman, *Trace of One*
Karen Volkman, *Spar*

2002
Lesle Lewis, *Small Boat*
Peter Jay Shippy, *Thieves' Latin*

2003
Michele Glazer, *Aggregate of Disturbances*
Dainis Hazners, *(some of) The Adventures of Carlyle, My Imaginary Friend*

2004
Megan Johnson, *The Waiting*
Susan Wheeler, *Ledger*

2005
Emily Rosko, *Raw Goods Inventory*
Joshua Marie Wilkinson, *Lug Your Careless Body out of the Careful Dusk*

2006
Elizabeth Hughey, *Sunday Houses the Sunday House*
Sarah Vap, *American Spikenard*

2008
andrew michael roberts, *something has to happen next*
Zach Savich, *Full Catastrophe Living*